The Journey of You

Unlocking Your Identity Through Erikson's Stages

Freudian Trips

Copyright Page

Published by Omniterra Media Inc

First Edition

Visit the author's website at www.freudiantrips.com

Disclaimer

The views and opinions expressed in this book are those of the author(s) and do not necessarily reflect the official policy or position of any other agency, organization, employer, or company. The contents of this book are for informational and educational purposes only and are not intended to serve as professional advice, diagnosis, or treatment.

The information provided in this book is believed to be accurate and reliable as of the date of publication. However, it may include some errors or inaccuracies, and no warranty or guarantee is provided regarding the accuracy, timeliness, or applicability of the content.

Readers are encouraged to consult with professional philosophers, educators, or other qualified professionals where appropriate for personalized advice. The author(s) and publisher shall not be liable for any loss, damage, or harm caused or alleged to be caused, directly or indirectly, by the information or ideas contained, suggested, or referenced in this book.

By reading this book, the reader acknowledges and agrees that they are solely responsible for how they interpret and apply the information contained herein.

This book may also include references to other works, studies, and sources. These references are provided for further reading and exploration and do not imply endorsement or validation of the specific theories, viewpoints, or interpretations presented in those works.

Introduction: Erik Erikson and the Map of Your Inner Journey

Picture your life as a long and winding road. Sometimes it's smooth, other times there are bumps and detours. Erik Erikson, a brilliant thinker in the world of psychology, believed that this journey of 'becoming yourself' has some predictable milestones along the way. He wasn't talking about learning to ride a bike or graduating from school. Erikson's milestones focus on our inner development.

Erikson had a fascinating background. While trained in the same tradition as the famous Sigmund Freud, he thought there was more to the story of human development than the psychosexual conflicts Freud emphasized. Erikson believed that how we relate to others, find our place in the world, and form a strong sense of who we are matters just as much. These are the building blocks of psychosocial development.

Now, why should you even care about all this? Because understanding Erikson's ideas is like having a compass for your inner journey. Every stage he described brings its own unique challenges and opportunities for growth. If you can figure out what stage you're working through, it's easier to navigate rough patches, gain confidence in the direction you're heading, and develop that rock-solid sense of self that makes life more fulfilling.

Key Points

- Erik Erikson was a psychologist who expanded traditional psychoanalytic ideas.
- Instead of focusing solely on internal desires, Erikson looked at how we develop within our social environment.
- His theory outlines eight stages of psychosocial development, each with its own crisis to overcome.
- Understanding Erikson's stages helps us gain self-awareness, navigate life's challenges, and build a strong identity.

Chapter 1: Baby Steps -- Trust vs. Mistrust

Imagine you're a tiny, brand new person. You can't walk, talk, or even focus your eyes properly. The world is a big, blurry, and sometimes scary place. But you're not alone! Your caregivers – parents, grandparents, or whoever steps up – are your lifeline. Erik Erikson believed this first stage of life is all about one central question: Can I trust the world around me?

The Building Blocks of Trust

When you cry because you're hungry, cold, or just need some snuggles, do the big people in your life come running? Do they soothe you with gentle voices and warm cuddles? If so, you're learning something incredibly important: the world is a safe place, and your needs will be met. This is the foundation of trust.

Of course, no caregiver is perfect. Sometimes there might be a little delay before you get fed, or your diaper change takes a bit longer. That's okay! As long as your needs are generally met with warmth and consistency, you're building that sense of security.

What if Things Don't Go So Smoothly?

Sadly, not all babies have the same experience. If caregivers are neglectful, inconsistent, or harsh, a baby might start to learn a very different lesson. The world might seem unpredictable or even dangerous. If their cries often go unanswered, they might develop a sense of mistrust, a deep unease that their needs won't be taken care of.

Why Does This Early Stage Matter So Much?

This first taste of trust or mistrust is like planting a seed. If a child feels secure and loved, they're more likely to grow into confident adults, able to build healthy relationships and explore the world. But, if early mistrust takes root, it can cast a long shadow. It becomes harder to form close bonds, anxiety might creep in, and there can be a nagging fear that things just won't work out.

The Good News

The human spirit is strong! Even if a baby has a rough start, it doesn't set their destiny in stone. With love, support, and perhaps some therapy later in life, those early patterns can be changed. Building strong relationships at any stage can help heal old wounds. Plus, Erikson's stages offer us a chance to check in with ourselves throughout life. Are we feeling that basic sense of safety in the world, or is there some lingering mistrust we need to work through?

Chapter Takeaway

The first year of life might seem like a blur, but it lays the foundation for our sense of self. Caregivers play a huge role in building either trust or mistrust. Luckily, love has immense power to heal, making growth and positive change possible at any age.

Chapter 2: "I Do It Myself!" – Autonomy vs. Shame and Doubt

Get ready for the toddler revolution! This stage of life is all about a brand new sense of "ME." Suddenly, these little people aren't just helpless babies. They're determined explorers with opinions of their own, and they want to try things their way. Erik Erikson saw this as a time of both thrilling discovery and a potential battleground between independence and the feeling of shame.

The Joy of "I Can!"

Picture a toddler proudly putting on their own shoes (even if they're backward!), choosing which shirt to wear, or trying to feed themselves with a spoon. Yes, it's messy, it's slow, and sometimes it looks like more food ends up on the floor. But this is monumental! Each of these attempts is a tiny declaration of independence, building the sense of "I can do things!"

Children at this stage are like little scientists, experimenting with cause and effect. What happens when they drop a toy?

Will the dog chase them if they giggle? It's all about exploring their power within the world around them.

When Independence Gets Tricky

Here's where parents, grandparents, and caregivers need the patience of saints! A toddler's newfound will doesn't always align with reality. They might want to wear shorts on a snowy day or decide that eating only cookies is a brilliant diet plan. This is where the tension between autonomy (their budding sense of control) and shame and doubt comes in.

How caregivers react in these moments is critical. If toddlers are constantly told "No!", scolded for making mistakes, or overly controlled, they might get this message: Your ideas are bad, and it's safer not to try. Over time, this can lead to shame and doubt around their own abilities.

The Power of Encouragement

The best caregivers find the delicate balance. They provide safe boundaries and gentle guidance (we can't wear bathing suits in winter!), but also lots of encouragement. Instead of doing everything for a toddler, they break down tasks into manageable steps. They celebrate those little wins, like successfully getting one sock on, even if it took ten minutes. This support fuels the child's belief in themselves and the joy of mastery.

Finding the Middle Ground

Perfect balance is rare, and we all lose our cool sometimes as caregivers. But, when toddlers feel generally supported in experimenting, with age-appropriate freedoms and limits, they learn an essential lesson. They can express themselves, make choices, and still be loved and accepted, even when they mess up.

Key Takeaways:

- Toddlers crave independence; it's exciting but also a bit scary for them.
- Caregivers who offer age-appropriate choices, encouragement, and safe boundaries help children develop a sense of healthy autonomy.
- Too much control can lead to feelings of shame and doubt.
- Just like babies, toddlers are also developing a sense of themselves in the world, but now with much more power to make choices!

Chapter 3: The Age of "Why?" – Initiative vs. Guilt

Get ready for a whirlwind of energy and a whole lot of questions! Early childhood is a time of massive curiosity and a growing desire to take charge. Erik Erikson called this the stage of Initiative vs. Guilt, a time when a child's sense of purpose starts to blossom, but it can also be a delicate balancing act for both kids and their caregivers.

The Power of Play

Preschool and kindergarten years are often filled with make-believe, building fantastic forts, and creating elaborate imaginary worlds. This isn't just about having fun (though fun is great!). Play is how children in this stage explore the world, try on different roles, and test the limits of their own abilities.

Imagine a child pretending to be a firefighter, bravely putting out a pretend blaze. They're learning about social roles, practicing problem-solving, and developing a sense of themselves as someone who can take action and help others. This is true initiative in action!

The Importance of Initiative

Kids of this age want to do things, start things, and make things happen! They have grand plans and ideas that might sometimes seem a bit outlandish to adults. This initiative is crucial for development. It's how they discover their interests, build confidence, and learn that they can have an impact on the world around them.

The Danger of Guilt

Sadly, initiative doesn't always get a positive reception. When kids are constantly told their ideas are silly, their plans won't work, or they're "too little" to do certain things, a different feeling can start to creep in: guilt. If children are harshly criticized, punished for making a mess, or micromanaged to the point where their own ideas don't matter, their sense of initiative can begin to wither.

Finding the Balance

This is where those patient caregivers come in once again. Children need safe space to try, explore, and sometimes fail. It's about setting up an environment where "Let's see if we can figure this out!" is the common phrase, instead of automatically jumping in to fix or rescue.

Messes can be cleaned up, some mistakes can be fixed, and kind redirection helps a child learn appropriate boundaries without crushing their spirit. Of course, this doesn't mean giving a four-year-old free reign in the kitchen with knives! It's about finding those areas where a child can safely explore with the right level of supervision.

Key Points:

- Early childhood is a time of boundless curiosity, creativity, and the desire to take action.
- Initiative grows through play, experimentation, and problem-solving opportunities.
- When a child's initiative is stifled, it can lead to feelings of guilt.
- Caregivers should create a space for safe exploration and healthy risk-taking, building confidence and a sense of purpose.

Chapter 4: Finding Your Spark – Industry vs. Inferiority

Remember those first days of "real" school? For some, those classrooms were exciting, filled with new things to learn and friends to make. For others, they might have felt a bit scary, a place where you were constantly measured and compared. Erik Erikson believed this school-age period is all about a child's growing sense of competence, and whether they feel "good enough" or not.

The Power of Doing

This stage is called Industry vs. Inferiority for a reason. Children now want to build things, master skills, and see what they can accomplish. Whether it's reading challenging books, learning a musical instrument, or excelling in a sport, they're driven by the desire to do things well.

Think of it like building a tower of blocks. Each new skill they learn, each project they complete, adds another block. That tower represents their growing competence, and it feels amazing! Pride in their work motivates them to keep learning and trying.

When Comparison Steals the Joy

Unfortunately, classrooms and playgrounds can also be breeding grounds for comparison. Kids are constantly getting messages, both subtle and not-so-subtle, about who is "smart," who is talented, and who always comes out on top.

When a child focuses too much on how they stack up against others, instead of their own progress, a sense of inferiority can start to creep in. It's that nagging feeling of "I'm not good enough," that fear of never measuring up. This can suck the joy out of learning and make kids want to avoid challenges, just to protect themselves from feeling like a failure.

The Role of Adults

Teachers, coaches, and of course, parents, play a massive role during this stage. The best ones focus on effort and improvement, not just the final outcome. They celebrate those small wins along the way, building a child's belief in their own ability to learn and grow.

It's crucial that adults help kids see that everyone has different strengths and that mistakes are a normal part of learning. It's tempting to compare our kids to others or fall into that trap of always talking about grades and test scores. But it's the love of learning and that sense of "I can do this!" attitude that fuels long-term success.

Key Takeaways:

- School-age kids crave accomplishment and the feeling of competence.
- Comparison to others can lead to feelings of inferiority and undermine a child's joy in learning.
- Adults should nurture a growth mindset, praising effort and progress, not just end results.
- This stage is about building skills and the confidence that comes with them – it's a foundation for future success!

Chapter 5: The "Who Am I?" Years – Identity vs. Role Confusion

If you think navigating toddlerhood is challenging, wait until you tackle adolescence! This stage is a storm of emotions, big questions, and some seriously confusing moments. Erik Erikson called it Identity vs. Role Confusion, and it perfectly describes the central struggle teenagers face as they try to figure out their place in the world.

Picture it Like This...

Imagine you've always been assigned a role in a play. You were the cute kid, the smart one, or maybe the class clown. But now, the play is over, and you get to rewrite your part! This is both thrilling and terrifying, which is pretty much how teenagers often feel.

Who Am I, Really?

This stage is all about answering that question: **Who am I?** Teenagers start diving into deeper topics, like their values, beliefs, future goals, and their unique personality. It is a moment of profound introspection, where individuals are reevaluating their knowledge of themselves and the world.

Trying on New Hats

Experimentation is the name of the game! Teens might try out different friend groups, clothing styles, hobbies, or even change their opinions from one week to the next. It might seem fickle to adults, but it all serves a purpose. It's like trying on a bunch of different hats to see which ones fit best.

This includes exploring roles within relationships, questions about gender identity and sexuality, as well as trying out different career paths in their imagination. There's a desire to define themselves as separate from their parents and family history.

The Power of Belonging

While figuring out that "me" part is crucial, teens also crave a strong sense of belonging. This is why friend groups become so important. These friendships offer a safe space to try out different sides of themselves, get feedback, and feel accepted for who they are, or at least, who they're becoming.

When Things Get Tricky

Not having a solid sense of self can feel like living in constant quicksand. This is what Erikson meant by role confusion. It can be incredibly disorienting and lead to anxiety or impulsive decisions in an attempt to fill the void.

Additionally, teens who don't feel supported, struggle to find a peer group where they belong, or who face discrimination face a much tougher journey in navigating this stage.

The Good News

Even though it feels messy, this identity exploration is essential! By challenging old assumptions and trying new things, teens lay the groundwork for a confident and self-aware adult life. Plus, adolescence is not a single event – it lasts for years, offering time to make adjustments and refine their sense of self.

Key takeaways:

- Teenagers are on a quest to define themselves, exploring values, beliefs, and potential roles they might play in life.
- Experimentation in everything from friends to fashion is a natural and healthy part of this stage.
- Having supportive peers and mentors helps teens feel less alone in this process.
- While this period can be tumultuous, it is vital for healthy adult development.

Chapter 6: The Intimacy Challenge – Love vs. Loneliness

Young adulthood is a time of exciting possibilities! Whether you're heading off to college, starting your dream career, or traveling the world, the horizon seems wider than ever before. But there's another major shift happening as well. Erik Erikson called it Intimacy vs. Isolation, and it's all about how we learn to form close, deep connections with others.

Love 101

Sure, there were crushes and maybe even some intense high school romances. But young adulthood is often when we start to think about love in a different way. This is about the desire to share your life with someone, to have a partner who truly knows you, the good, the bad, and the embarrassing! However, it's not just about romantic love; it includes deep friendships and strong family bonds as well.

Finding Your People

Remember those friends you made in the sandbox? Chances are, some of those friendships have faded, while new ones have blossomed. As a young adult, you get to be more selective about who you surround yourself with. These connections are built on shared interests, similar values, and a real sense of understanding each other deeply.

Building intimacy is about being vulnerable, opening up, and truly letting yourself be seen. It's a big risk, and everyone has some fear of being hurt or rejected. But the reward is immeasurable!

Loneliness – The Other Side of the Coin

If building deep connections is the goal, then the flip side is isolation. When young adults struggle to form those strong bonds, whether due to shyness, moving around a lot, or past hurts, it can lead to a deep sense of loneliness. This doesn't always look like being alone in a room. You can feel isolated even when surrounded by casual acquaintances or in a romantic relationship that lacks true connection.

The Balancing Act

There's also a delicate dance happening in this stage. While we are longing for intimacy, part of us might still crave that youthful independence. How do we balance a strong sense of "me" along with a shared "us" in a relationship? Finding that perfect balance takes time and conscious effort.

Key Takeaways:

- Young adulthood is a time for forming deep, meaningful relationships of all kinds.
- Building intimacy requires vulnerability and overcoming the fear of rejection.

- Isolation can occur even when surrounded by people, it's about the quality of the connections.
- Relationships in this stage influence our sense of self, and it's essential to find a balance between independence and interdependence.

Chapter 7: Finding Your Mark - Generativity vs. Stagnation

Remember when you were a kid, and adults asked, "What do you want to be when you grow up?" Middle adulthood brings up a similar question: **What do you want your life to mean?** Erik Erikson captured this perfectly in his stage of **Generativity vs. Stagnation.**

Beyond the Self

This stage is a shift in focus. It's about looking beyond our own immediate needs and finding ways to nurture and guide the next generation. This could mean being an amazing parent, a dedicated mentor at work, volunteering in your community, or getting involved in causes you believe in.

Generativity comes in many forms. It's about making a contribution to the world that will outlast your individual lifetime. It leaves a legacy – children raised with love, knowledge passed on, communities made stronger, and that satisfying feeling of having made a difference.

Feeling Stuck - The Risk of Stagnation

The flip side of generativity is stagnation. This feels like being stuck on a treadmill, going through the motions without a sense of real purpose. Maybe it's a mid-life crisis caused by a boring job, a stale relationship, or the realization that some youthful dreams will never come true. This stagnation can lead to boredom, bitterness, and a sense of emptiness.

Mid-Course Correction

The good news is, middle adulthood is a time for taking stock and making changes if needed! Erikson didn't believe we're locked into any stage for life. Perhaps it's taking night classes to pursue a career change, rekindling old passions and hobbies, or discovering new ways to give back to your community.

Generativity is a muscle that needs exercise. Sometimes it might feel like a major shift, other times small acts of kindness can create a ripple effect. The key is to find what makes you feel connected to something larger than yourself.

Shifting Values

It's also common for our values to shift during this stage. Things that once seemed all-important, like chasing ever-higher salaries or a fancier house, might suddenly lose their appeal. Instead, experiences, meaningful relationships, and making an impact on others often climb to the top of our priority list.

Key Takeaways:

- Middle adulthood is a time when many people seek ways to leave a positive legacy.

- Generativity involves contributing to the next generation or finding ways to make the world a better place.
- Stagnation occurs when a person feels stuck in a rut, without a sense of purpose.
- This stage is a great time to reassess life goals and values, making changes as needed.
- Generativity is a choice we can actively make at any point in our lives.

Chapter 8: Reflections – Ego Integrity vs. Despair

Imagine your life as a long movie reel. As you reach late adulthood, Erik Erikson believed it's natural to start reviewing that movie, looking back on the twists and turns, the triumphs and disappointments. This is his final stage: **Ego Integrity vs. Despair.**

Making Peace with the Past

Ego integrity means looking back on your life with a sense of acceptance. It's not about having a perfect life – everyone makes mistakes and has regrets. But it's about coming to terms with your choices, finding meaning in the journey, and feeling a sense of peace about the person you've become.

This stage involves a whole lot of reflection. It might mean flipping through old photo albums, reconnecting with people from your past, or journaling about your experiences. The goal is to weave the different parts of your life into a whole story that makes sense.

The Sting of Despair

On the flip side is despair. This is when looking back brings mostly feelings of deep regret, missed opportunities, or bitterness. It's that nagging feeling of "if only I had...," Despair can arise when someone feels they haven't lived a fulfilling life or that they can't repair past hurts.

The Wisdom of Age

Late adulthood is a time when many people gain profound wisdom. Having weathered life's storms brings perspective that younger folks don't always possess. Seniors who have reached ego integrity often become incredible sources of advice, support, and inspiration for younger generations. If they can share their hard-won wisdom, it furthers that sense of leaving a positive legacy.

It's Never Too Late

Remember, Erikson didn't see these stages as set in stone. If an older adult is struggling with despair, therapy can help them work through past regrets and find more peace in the present. It's also possible to find new purpose at this stage, through volunteer work, creative projects, or simply focusing on building strong relationships with loved ones.

The End of the Story

Late adulthood naturally brings thoughts of our own mortality. Finding integrity means coming to terms with the fact that our life story won't go on forever. It's about finding peace and meaning even at life's close.

Key Takeaways:

- Late adulthood is a time for looking back and evaluating one's life journey.
- Ego integrity means feeling a sense of peace and acceptance about your life, despite imperfections.
- Despair can arise from deep regrets or a feeling that life lacked meaning.
- Wisdom is a common gift of late adulthood, and sharing it can contribute to a sense of purpose.
- It's never too late to make changes and find greater fulfillment in life, even in old age.

Chapter 9: The Journey Continues – Lessons from Erikson

Picture your life not as a straight line, but as a winding path full of detours and hidden turnoffs. Some parts might be smooth sailing, others a rocky uphill climb. This is more like how Erik Erikson saw our development. His stages offer a framework for reflection, not a rigid checklist we have to complete in a specific order.

No Deadlines for Growth

One of the most empowering things about Erikson's theory is that it's never too late for change. Maybe you struggled with building trust as a child, or you're feeling a bit stuck and unfulfilled in middle adulthood. Understanding Erikson's stages can spark a lightbulb moment: Aha, this is what I've been wrestling with!

Once we have awareness, it's far easier to take action. Therapy, developing new skills, or strengthening relationships can all help us work through challenges, even years after that specific stage has passed.

Tools for Your Journey

Think of Erikson's stages like signposts to help you navigate the journey of self-discovery. Here are a few self-reflection questions based on each stage to get you started:

- **Trust vs. Mistrust:** Do I have a fundamental sense of safety and trust in the world? If not, what experiences might have impacted that?
- **Autonomy vs. Shame and Doubt:** Do I feel confident in my abilities? Am I sometimes held back by fear of failure?
- **Initiative vs. Guilt:** Am I proactive in taking charge of my life, or do I often wait for things to happen to me?
- **Industry vs. Inferiority:** Do I feel competent? What makes me feel accomplished and proud?
- **Identity vs. Role Confusion:** Who am I, deep down? What are my core values and beliefs?
- **Intimacy vs. Isolation:** Do I have deep, meaningful connections with others? How can I nurture those bonds further?
- **Generativity vs. Stagnation:** Am I contributing to something larger than myself? What kind of legacy do I want to leave?
- **Ego Integrity vs. Despair:** When I look back, do I feel mostly at peace with my life? What still causes feelings of regret?

A Lifelong Process

Remember, self-development is messy and ongoing. There's no finish line to cross! Be kind to yourself as you reflect on

Erikson's stages. Even small steps, like journaling, exploring a new hobby, or having a heart-to-heart with a loved one, can lead to growth and a stronger sense of purpose at any point in your life.

Key Takeaways:

- Erikson's theory is a guide for understanding your life's journey, not a rigid set of rules.
- Positive change is possible at any age. Awareness of Erikson's stages can help spark that change.
- Use self-reflection questions to gain insight into your past experiences and present needs at each stage.
- Your path is unique – embrace the detours, celebrate the milestones, and never stop exploring who you are!

About Freudian Trips

Welcome to Freudian Trips, your dedicated platform for diving deep into the world of psychology. We are more than just a YouTube channel or a book publisher. We are a beacon of enlightenment, making complex psychological concepts accessible and engaging for all.

Our YouTube channel is a rich repository of psychology made simple. We take the profound and often complex ideas from the world of psychology and break them down into digestible, easy-to-understand content. From the foundational theories of Freud to the cognitive insights of Piaget, we cover a broad spectrum of psychological schools and thoughts, making psychology accessible to everyone, regardless of their background or prior knowledge.

As a book publisher, we take the same approach, transforming intricate psychological theories into comprehensible narratives. Our books are not just collections of words, but vessels of wisdom that make psychology approachable and relatable. We believe that psychology should not be confined to academic circles, but should be available to all who seek to understand the human mind and behavior.

At Freudian Trips, we believe in the power of curiosity and the pursuit of knowledge. We are here to stoke the fires of your curiosity, to guide you on your intellectual journey, and to help you navigate the fascinating world of psychology.

If you are someone who is not afraid to question, to explore, and to learn, then you are in the right place. Join us on this journey of exploration, as we make psychology easy to understand, one concept at a time.

Be sure to visit our Youtube channel at:
www.freudiantrips.com/youtube

You can also visit us on the web at www.freudiantrips.com

Welcome to The Freudian Trip community. Stay curious. Stay enlightened.